Understanding

Your

Constitution

Book 1

Dr. Yi Song

ISBN: 979-8-9948506-2-6 (print)

This is Book One of

Regeneration Effect :

Sacred Wisdom for Staying Young

BOOK 1

No matter how much we want to

believe otherwise, the reality is that

the human lifespan has always had its

limits. Even over 6,000 years ago, in

the *Huangdi Neijing*—the Yellow

Emperor's Classic of Medicine—the

ancient Chinese sages acknowledged

this truth. They wrote that the

maximum human lifespan is around

120 years, and that hasn't changed, even today.

One story that's stayed with me is of a Taoist practitioner who lived well past 100, walking mountain paths daily, preparing his own meals, teaching younger students not just about herbs or acupuncture, but about presence.

He said, "If you chase youth, it will always run from you. But if you live gently and wisely, youth will return in unexpected ways."

I never forgot that.

Today, our approach is so different. We're obsessed with pushing back the clock—freezing time with cryotherapy, reversing it with stem cells, buying it with supplements, creams, and cold plunges. We're exhausted, bloated, irritable, unable to sleep without pills. Our joints ache. Our digestion is a mess. We don't laugh much.

We've been taught to fight against age instead of flow with life. To manage symptoms instead of nurture balance. I'm here to show you ways to keep yourself happy and healthy with the right tools. Take medications for cholesterol, supplements that will help you more than Western civilization methods.

To me, true vitality lives beyond the lab reports.

It lives in the way your body wakes up in the morning. In how deeply you sleep. In whether you can climb stairs without wincing. In the sound of your own laughter. In the ability to move, breathe, eat, and feel without discomfort. **That's what matters. That's what lasts.**

Reaching 120 in good health depends on many factors—your constitution, your habits, and your genetic makeup.

Yet the guidance offered by the sage

T'ien Shih still holds true today:

Practice self-care, rest deeply, eat mindfully, seek inner contentment, and cultivate joy that lasts.

It's not about resisting nature. It's about working with it so we can age with strength, clarity, and vitality.

As we age, our constitutional energy —our core vitality, that deep inner spark we're born with—naturally begins to decline. **It's like a reservoir we draw from every day**. Some people are born with a deep, wide well. Others start with less—maybe due to genetics, early childhood conditions, or unresolved trauma. But no matter how much you start with, the flow eventually lessens.

If your reservoir was already shallow, **even a normal rate of depletion can leave you feeling "old" far earlier than expected**—tired, sluggish, more prone to illness or pain. I've seen it in people who never had a fair start. They're doing their best, but the tank was half-empty before life really began.

But here's the beautiful part:

While you may not be able to change the size of your reservoir, you *can* learn how to protect what's left.

You can stop the leaks. You can seal the cracks. You can even create small streams that replenish your well—through **rest, nourishment, movement, and stillness.**

The real secret isn't about defying age; it's about *harmonizing* with it.

Supporting the body's natural

rhythms, replenishing what's been lost, and **slowing the decline rather than chasing an illusion.** Instead of focusing on unattainable immortality, this chapter guides you to:

- **Accept your body's natural limitations** while working to strengthen and optimize your constitution.

- **Embrace longevity strategies** that slow decline without denying the reality of aging.

- **Shift the goal** from endless life to a full, vibrant, and meaningful one.

Understanding your health means seeing both the forest and the trees—the big picture and the small, intricate pieces that make you who you are. Your body isn't just a reflection of what you eat or how much you exercise; it's an ongoing story shaped by generations before you and the choices you make every day.

Recently, I took a DNA test. With the advancement of human genome research, we can now see, to a certain extent, how our genes influence not only our physical health but also our mood and emotional tendencies. Nature and nurture both matter, but DNA lays the foundation for how we interact with the world. What amazed me was how accurate the results were —almost 90% spot on—even though the testers knew nothing about me.

The report revealed traits that explained so much about my own constitution: tendencies to overthink, to feel overstimulated, to process the world in a certain rhythm. It reminded me that knowing your body's blueprint—your genetic constitution—isn't about being limited by it. It's about understanding how to work *with* it. Once you know your inherent patterns, you can choose practices like meditation, specific forms of exercise, or diet changes to balance what nature gave you.

I saw this clearly in one of my clients. His son, only twenty-seven, was suddenly diagnosed with hypertension. The family was puzzled—was it hereditary? His wife was on medication, but his case seemed too early, too severe. When we looked deeper, it became clear that the real trigger wasn't just genetic—it was emotional. He was in the middle of a stressful divorce, and his blood pressure was his body's way of expressing that turmoil. Genes can set the stage, but life circumstances determine how those genes are expressed. Stress, diet, and emotional patterns all act like switches—turning tendencies on or off.

My own family carries a similar story.

My grandmother had diabetes, and my mother was diagnosed with pre-diabetes in her fifties. A few years ago, my DNA test confirmed I also carry the same genetic markers. But genes aren't destiny—they're potential. When my mother learned about her risk, we made changes early. She adjusted her diet, avoided refined carbs and sugars, and began using herbal formulas to stabilize her blood sugar. Over time, her pre-diabetes reversed completely.

She's now eighty-one, vibrant and active, with no trace of diabetes. Even the inflammation in her legs—once so severe that they swelled red like "Christmas stockings"—has subsided. Western doctors suggested vein ablation or stents, procedures that often worsen circulation or create more blockages. Instead, she chose a regenerative path. After three stem cell treatments and continued natural support, her circulation improved, and her legs healed without surgery.

Her journey is proof that understanding both the big picture and the details—your DNA, your emotions, your lifestyle, and your mindset—can change the trajectory of your health. You inherit more than genes; you inherit patterns. But with awareness, you can rewrite how those patterns express themselves.

Valerie Orsoni was another person who left a strong impression on me. A well-known biohacker, wellness expert, and bestselling author, she's built a reputation on grounding longevity and nutrition in solid science.

Like my first client, Valerie isn't free from life's pressures. She deals with her own challenges, responsibilities, and internal storms. But rather than burying them or pretending they don't exist, she's devoted years to understanding how her mind and body respond, and finding ways to channel those tendencies into strength. Over time, that consistency hasn't just helped her manage stress—it's allowed her to thrive.

Understanding your constitution isn't about labeling yourself or limiting your potential. It's about recognizing your patterns so you can work *with* your body instead of against it.

If you were born with a **weaker digestive system**, iced drinks and raw salads may not support your energy. Instead, warm soups, lightly cooked vegetables, and herbs like ginger or cinnamon may strengthen your core.

If you tend toward **excess heat**—you break out easily, get red in the face, feel irritable or restless—you don't need more stimulation. You need to cool the system down. That might mean peppermint tea instead of coffee, time in nature instead of a second HIIT class.

Cryotherapy is a great example— some walk away feeling charged and clear, while others feel cold, fatigued, or energetically off for hours. Food works the same way; some people thrive on plant-based proteins, while others feel inflamed, sluggish, or nutrient-deficient when relying on them as a primary source.

Now, that doesn't mean what I do

would work for everyone. But that's

exactly the point. It's not about

following what someone else is doing.

It's about **figuring out what works**

for your body and building from there.

My Mother's Constitution Story

I remember the moment we realized that my mom's diet had to change. We needed to make it more **cholesterol-friendly.** Not just for her well-being, but for her future. My mom grew up during a time of famine. Those early years shaped her relationship with food in a deep, emotional way. **She had lived through scarcity,** and that kind of deprivation doesn't just disappear. It leaves a mark.

When I was about 20, it was the late 1990s. That's when things began to shift. **Suddenly, we had access to a whole new world of food.** Grocery stores were stocked with variety, shelves were lined with bright packaging and flavors we hadn't grown up with. For my mom, it was like stepping into another world. After years of limitation, now she could try anything. And she did. She was curious. She was excited. And honestly, she became hooked.

She gravitated toward Western processed foods, the kind you might consider junk food. Snack cakes, sugary cereals, fast food. They were new and exciting to her, and she embraced them with a sense of freedom and joy. But over time, this new diet started to take a toll.

Then came a health scare. Bleeding in her fovea. That was the turning point. It was serious, and it forced all of us to take a step back and reevaluate. We had to have some hard conversations with her. We told her gently but firmly: you can't eat like this anymore. No more of this, none of that. It was tough, but **she started to become more conscious of what she put in her body.**

We introduced her to healthier options. Whole grains, fresh vegetables, foods lower in saturated fats. **One of the things we used was red yeast rice.** It wasn't a miracle cure, of course, but it became part of a broader strategy to help her rebuild her health. And since making those changes, she hasn't had high cholesterol again. Not even to this day.

But I want to be clear: it wasn't just about the rice. I'm not saying, "Hey, throw this one food into your diet and everything will be perfect." That's never how it works. That's just one piece of the puzzle. You have to combine everything. **Nutrition,**

movement, mental wellness, habits, purpose. You can't single out one practice and expect it to carry the weight of your entire health journey.

This really speaks to the holistic approach to aging and health that I believe in. **No single thing will solve everything.** Just like stem cell therapy won't magically fix all aging problems. It's never about one magic bullet. **You have to take care of your whole self. Layer by layer, day by day.**

Remember, your constitution isn't a life sentence. It's a starting point.

With awareness and appropriate support, you can strengthen your weaknesses and balance your excesses. The goal isn't to change who you are. It's to become the healthiest version of yourself.

Your body already knows what it needs.

Recognize your body's unique constitution and address your particular strength and weakness with methods suitable to your unique body, not just using cookie-cutter one-size-fits-all approaches.

To find your body's unique constitution, arrange a private consultation with Dr. Yi Song. Many people seek advice from different experts including talking to different clinics offering advanced stem cell therapy. A lot of people find Dr. Yi Song has her unique intuition to decipher what underlying imbalance causes the symptoms and give you advice on approaches very different from conventional Western medicine doctors or other holistic practitioners. Holistic approach is not just putting together trendy alternative therapies. Truly holistic approach requires a deep understanding of the interconnectedness of different parts of the body and view the body as a garden instead of a machine. You are welcome to read about the principles about "Treat Your Body as a Garden", "Treat the Root Cause of Imbalance and Disease". Scan the QR code to get on the journey of recognizing your

own body's unique constitution.

To get in-depth discussion about your unique constitution, please follow the link or scan the QR code to preorder "Regeneration Effect: Sacred Wisdom for Staying Young" and learn how you can implement all the principles in your life.

https://bundle.regenerationeffect.com

ABOUT THE AUTHOR

Dr. Yi Song was born and raised in Beijing, China, into a family with seventeen generations of experience in both Chinese and Western medicine. Twenty-eight years ago, she came to the United States to study pathology at Brown University. After observing the shortcomings of symptom-focused treatments, Dr. Song returned to her roots to focus on true regenerative healing — addressing disease at its source. She has had a holistic clinic in Boston since 2004. In 2018, she founded the Zenerchi Retreat in Medellin, Colombia. Her introduction to stem cell therapy in 2020 was marked by her mother's successful treatment and subsequent independence at age 81. Dr. Song believes that stem cell therapy aligns with holistic principles and is the author of "Regeneration Effect: Sacred Wisdom for Staying Young" and the series of seven books in "The Six Principles to Natural Longevity". Her vision is to combine stem cell therapy, Traditional Chinese Medicine, and anti-aging treatments to help people live a long, high-quality life. She offers advanced stem cell treatments at Zenerchi Retreat in Colombia not available in the US. You can also get consultation about your conditions and concerns in person in Boston or at our network of doctors in the US and online.

9 798994 850626